Legal Essentials

Disability Discrimination

Hammond Suddards Edge

Chartered Institute of Personnel and Development

© Hammond Suddards Edge 2000
First published 2000
Reprinted 2000

Design and typesetting by Beacon GDT, Ruardean, Gloucestershire.
Printed in Great Britain by the Cromwell Press, Trowbridge, Wiltshire.

British Library Cataloguing in Publication Data
A catalogue record for this book is available from the British Library

ISBN 0 85292 855 6

The views expressed in the book are the authors' own and may not necessarily
reflect those of the CIPD. Although the CIPD has made every effort to ensure
that the information in this book is both accurate and up to date, the Institute
accepts no responsibility for any errors or omissions. It should be noted that
ultimately only the courts can interpret the law. The law in this book is stated as
at March 2000.

Throughout this publication the male gender has, in general, been used for
convenience, but it should be read to include the female gender.

Chartered Institute of Personnel and Development
CIPD House, Camp Road, London SW19 4UX
Telephone 020 8971 9000 Facsimile 020 8263 3333
E-mail: cipd@cipd.co.uk Website: www.cipd.co.uk
Incorporated by Royal Charter. Registered charity no. 1079797

Contents

The authors

Hammond Suddards Edge run the popular legal advisory service for CIPD members, which takes literally thousands of calls a month from practitioners worried about the legal implications of their job. Most of those calls are concerned with the issues covered by this series. Judith Firth, legal adviser on the CIPD legal advisory service, and Hammond Suddards Edge partner and Head of Employment Unit Susan Nickson write from extensive experience in the area of employment law. Judith will also be familiar to readers of *People Management* magazine for her regular column on employment law issues.

List of abbreviations

LEGISLATION

DDA   *Disability Discrimination Act 1995*
ERA   *Employment Rights Act 1996*
RRA   *Race Relations Act 1976*
SDA   *Sex Discrimination Act 1975*

COURTS

CA   *Court of Appeal*
EAT   *Employment Appeal Tribunal*

CASE REFERENCES

ICR   *Industrial Case Reports*
IRLR   *Industrial Relations Law Reports*

SHORT FORMS

ACAS   *Advisory, Conciliation and Arbitration Service*
CRE   *Commission for Racial Equality*
DfEE   *Department for Education and Employment*
DRC   *Disability Rights Commission*
DRTF   *Disability Rights Task Force*
EOC   *Equal Opportunities Commission*
IT   *information technology*
SOSR   *some other substantial reason*
& ors   *and others*
t/a   *trading as*

List of legislation cited

Note: page numbers refer to first reference only

List of cases cited

Note: page numbers refer to first reference only

Frequently asked questions

What is the purpose of the employment provisions of the Disability Discrimination Act 1995 ('the Act')?

To make it unlawful to discriminate against a disabled person at any stage of employment.

What does 'at any stage of employment' mean?

- the arrangements made for the purpose of determining who should be offered that employment

- in the terms on which employment is offered

- by refusing or deliberately omitting to offer employment

- in the opportunities for promotion, training or the receipt of any other benefit

- dismissal or subjection to any other detriment. [DDA s4]

Who is covered by the employment provisions of the Act?

All persons who have a disability and who are employed under a contract of service or of apprenticeship or a contract for personal service, except:

- those whose employer has fewer than 15 full- or part-time employees

- prison officers, firefighters, members of a police force

- employees who work wholly or mainly outside Great Britain

- members of the Armed Forces

- people who work on board ships, aircraft or hovercraft.

What is the definition of 'Disability'?

A person has a disability if he or she has a physical or mental impairment which has a substantial and long-term adverse effect on his or her ability to carry out normal day-to-day activities. [DDA s1 (1)]

When does an impairment affect a person's ability to carry out normal day-to-day activities?

When it affects one of the following:

- mobility

- manual dexterity

- physical co-ordination

- continence

- the ability to lift, carry or otherwise move everyday objects

- speech, hearing or eyesight

- memory or ability to concentrate, learn or understand

- perception of the risk of physical danger. [DDA sch 4(1)]

What constitutes 'long-term'?

The effect of an impairment is long-term if one of the following is true:

- It has lasted for 12 months.

- It is likely to last for 12 months.

- It is likely to last for the rest of that person's life.

- It is likely to reoccur if it is currently in remission. [DDA sch 2 (1)(2)]

How do you show that the effect of the impairment is substantial?

It is a question of fact for the tribunal to decide. Factors to take into account include the following:

- the time taken to carry out the task

- the way in which the task is carried out

- the cumulative effects of the impairment

- the effect of the environment on the impairment

- the extent to which it is reasonable for the disabled person to modify his behaviour in order to minimise the effect of the impairment.

In what ways can an employer be guilty of discriminating against a disabled person?

By:

- directly discriminating

- failing to make a reasonable adjustment

- victimisation.

What is direct discrimination?

An employer directly discriminates against a disabled person if, for a reason that relates to the disabled person's disability, the employer treats the disabled person less favourably than he treats or would treat others to whom that reason does not or would not apply, and the employer cannot show that the treatment is justified for a material and substantial reason. [DDA s5 (1)]

What is discrimination by way of failure to make reasonable adjustments?

An employer is under a duty to take such steps as are reasonable to prevent (a) any arrangements made by him or on his behalf, or (b) any physical features of the employer's premises from placing a disabled applicant or employee at a substantial disadvantage to non-disabled applicants or employees.

Consequently an employer discriminates against a disabled person by way of failure to make reasonable adjustments if:

- the employer fails to take such reasonable steps, and

- the employer cannot show that the failure is justified for a material and substantial reason. [DDA s6 (1)]

What does 'reasonable' mean?

The DDA lists a number of factors that may have a bearing on whether it will be reasonable for the employer to have to make a particular adjustment. These are:

- the effectiveness of the particular adjustment in preventing the disadvantage

- the practicability of the adjustment

- the financial and other costs of the adjustment and the extent of any disruption caused

- the extent of the employer's financial and other resources and

- the availability to the employer of financial or other assistance to help make an adjustment.

What steps need to be taken?

Steps that employers may have to take to prevent arrangements or premises placing people with disabilities at a substantial disadvantage are:

- making adjustments to premises

- allocating some of the disabled person's duties to another person

- transferring the person to fill an existing vacancy

- altering the person's working hours

- assigning the person to a different place of work

- allowing absences during working hours for rehabilitation, assessment or treatment

- giving or arranging training for the person

- acquiring or modifying equipment

- modifying instructions or reference manuals

- modifying procedures for testing or assessment

- providing a reader or interpreter

- providing supervision.

What is discrimination by way of victimisation?

An employer discriminates against a disabled person by way of victimisation if:

- the employer treats the disabled person less favourably than he treats or would treat other persons whose circumstances are the same as the disabled person's (disregarding the disability) and does so because the disabled person intends to, has or is believed to have:

(a) brought proceedings against anyone under the Act; or

(b) given evidence or information in connection with such proceedings brought by any person; or

(c) otherwise done anything to anyone under the Act; or

(d) alleged that the Act has been contravened by anyone. [DDA s 55]

NB A person is not protected under (d) where the allegation is false and not made in good faith.

What happens if the employer does not know that the applicant or employee is disabled?

The Act does not impose any duty upon the employer in relation to a disabled person if the employer does not know and could not reasonably be expected to know that the person has a disability. [DDA s 6 (6)(b)]

What happens if an employee believes that he has been discriminated against on the grounds of disability?

The employee may make a complaint to an employment tribunal *within 3 months* from when the discrimination took place.

Where a complaint is upheld, an employment tribunal may then:

- declare the rights of the parties involved

- recommend that the employer take reasonable action, within a specified time, to prevent or reduce the adverse effect on the complainant of the discrimination or of the failure to make an adjustment

- order the respondent to pay compensation to the claimant.

Sample disabled workers policy

This is an example of a basic disabled workers policy that an employer ('the Company') may adopt. The policy is for illustrative purposes only and will require 'tailoring' to the needs of the specific employer and his workforce.

As an equal opportunities employer, the Company wishes to ensure that no employee or applicant for employment with the Company suffers unjustifiable discrimination because of his or her disability. The Company will therefore follow procedures designed to provide that all employees and applicants are treated on the basis of their relative merits.

In particular, the Company will not discriminate in the recruitment of employees, the terms and conditions afforded to employees, promotion, training or any other benefit afforded to employees, or in the disciplining of employees, in a way that does or may discriminate against disabled employees.

When employees become disabled during their employment, steps will be taken, through retraining or redeployment if necessary, to enable employees to remain in employment with the Company whenever possible.

Any employee who believes that he or she has been discriminated against or that a colleague has suffered discrimination should raise the matter under the grievance procedure. [*NB Consider appointing a Disabled Workers Officer or someone similar to whom complaints should be made, or consider appointing someone who is to be involved in the grievance procedure.*] Employees are assured that any complaints will be dealt with in confidence and will be regarded with the utmost seriousness.

Employees should be aware that under the Disability Discrimination Act 1995 a disabled person is someone who has (or had) an impairment that substantially affects his or her ability to do everyday activities over a sustained period. Progressive conditions such as multiple sclerosis, cancer, HIV/AIDS, together with speech and hearing defects, are likely to amount to a disability as well as more obvious mental and physical handicaps such as paraplegia.

The Company regards unlawful discrimination against any employee (whether disabled or not) as a disciplinary matter, but certainly any employee(s) who breach this policy will be dealt with under the disciplinary procedure and may well be dismissed for gross misconduct.

Introduction

The Disability Discrimination Act 1995 (DDA) received Royal Assent on 8 November 1995 and the employment provisions came into force on 2 December 1996. It is the first piece of legislation to address disability-related discrimination in the UK. A labour force survey in 1994–5 compiled statistics which showed that there were 3.8 million disabled adults below pensionable age in Great Britain, 1.2 million disabled people in employment, and that the unemployment level for disabled people was twice that of non-disabled.

Prior to the passing of the DDA there had been no legislative strategy to tackle disability discrimination. The Disabled Persons (Employment) Act 1944 had operated a quota system whereby employers who had 20 or more employees were under a duty to employ a quota of 3 per cent of their workforce of registered disabled people. It was rarely enforced, and although the government advocated voluntary good practice, this did not give disabled people redress at law should they be discriminated against because of their disability.

Much of the campaigning for legislation to deal with disability discrimination focused on the measures introduced by other countries, particularly the USA with the Disabilities Act 1990. As a result of mounting pressure, in July 1994 the government published a consultation document which was followed in January 1995 by a White Paper, and thereafter the Disability Discrimination Bill was published. The DDA has received much criticism as a confusing and complicated piece of legislation, as a result of which a code of practice and formal guidance have been issued. Case law has also played its part in interpreting legislation, as is the case with other discrimination legislation which has been with us now for a quarter of a century. Comparisons between the Sex Discrimination Act 1975 (SDA) and the Race Relations Act 1976 (RRA) are inevitable as a means of guidance, but there are significant differences. For example, there is no concept of indirect discrimination under the DDA, and employers with fewer than 15 employees are excluded. Additionally, direct discrimination under the DDA may be justified. Under the SDA and the RRA this is possible only in relation to indirect discrimination. This distinction is on the basis that a disability may be relevant to a person's ability to perform work, unlike a person's race or sex (other than in the context of a genuine occupational qualification).

The purpose of this guide is to provide a summary of the main areas of the DDA and to provide assistance in identifying relevant case law and practical examples of its applicability in the workplace. Greater awareness of legal rights means that cases brought before employment tribunals have increased dramatically. In 1998 the number of disability discrimination cases dealt with by ACAS doubled to 2,758, compared with an increase of just over 4 per cent in sex discrimination cases and 10 per cent in race discrimination cases.

Chapter 1 of the guide identifies and examines the definition of disability, while Chapter 2 deals with the question of the scope of the protection and liability. Chapter 3 shows the practical application of the legislation and Chapter 4 the area of reasonable adjustments. Chapter 5 identifies the mechanism for making a claim and, finally, Chapter 6 identifies the developments that we are likely to see in this area of law. On page xiv is an example of a disabled workers policy.

The definition of disability

Requirements of the statutory definition – *Impairment –
Substantial adverse effect – Long term – Normal day-to-day
activities – Conditions that have been held to amount to a disability*

The purpose of this chapter is to examine the definition of disability
and the statutory guidance that has been provided.

Under section 1(1) of the DDA a person has a disability 'if he has a
physical or *mental impairment* which has a *substantial* and *long-term
adverse effect* on his ability to carry out *normal day-to-day activities*.'

The burden is on the applicant to show he satisfies the requirements of
the section 1 definition. A disabled person is a person who *has* a disability,
but also a person who *has had* a disability. In other words, past disabilities
that a person has suffered from are included under the protection of the
DDA.

Under section 3 of the DDA, the Secretary of State has issued guidance
to assist in determining whether an illness is a disability – 'Guidance to
be taken into account in determining questions relating to the definition
of disability' ('the Guidance'). Section 3(3) of the DDA states that, in
determining whether an impairment has a substantial and long-term
adverse effect on a person's ability to carry out normal day-to-day
activities, a tribunal or court shall take into account the contents of the
guidance that appear to be relevant. It is therefore important for all
employers to be familiar with its provisions.

Before examining the statutory definition in more detail it should be
noted that there are conditions that are specifically excluded from the
definition of disability and therefore the scope of the DDA, and these
are listed in the Guidance as:

- addiction to or dependency on alcohol, nicotine, or any other
  substance (other than in consequence of the substance being
  medically prescribed)

- the condition known as seasonal allergic rhinitis (eg hay fever) except where it aggravates the effect of another condition

- a tendency to set fires

- a tendency to steal

- a tendency to physical or sexual abuse of other persons

- exhibitionism

- voyeurism

- disfigurements such as tattoos or body-piercing.

REQUIREMENTS OF THE STATUTORY DEFINITION

Impairment

This may be a physical or mental impairment. Although the conditions listed above are excluded, a condition arising as a result of one of these conditions may be a disability, such as liver disease arising as a result of alcohol dependency.

Physical

There is little guidance on the meaning of physical impairment, mainly because there will generally be no dispute whether a person has an impairment or not. However, by way of example, case-law has shown that back injuries may be included as a physical impairment. In the case of *Sillifant* v *North & East Devon Health Authority* (Case No. 1401241/97) the applicant was an office manager who injured her back in a fall while on holiday in August 1996. The applicant was due to return to work in March 1997 but suffered a muscle spasm. The applicant was told by her doctor that she would be fit to return in six weeks, although she failed to communicate this to her employer and advised them that she did not know when she would return. The employee was dismissed by the employer on the basis that they could not longer cope with her absences. The employee made a claim of unlawful discrimination under the DDA. Although the tribunal dismissed her claim because the employer's actions were justified, what was pertinent was that the tribunal, having heard medical evidence as to the nature of the applicant's injury, found that she had suffered muscle and ligament tendon damage of a kind that generally takes two years to mend and that she therefore had a physical impairment.

Mental

A mental impairment under schedule 1 of the DDA must be a clinically well-recognised illness. This is an illness that is recognised by a respected body of medical opinion. This includes those stated in the World Health Organization's International Classification of Diseases, eg schizophrenia and manic depression.

Substantial adverse effect

This means more than trivial or minor. It is the effect that the impairment has – not the severity of the impairment itself – that is relevant. Paragraphs A1 to A17 of the Guidance deal with the question of what a substantial adverse effect is. Factors that may be taken into consideration in deciding whether an impairment has a substantial adverse effect include:

- the time to be taken by a person with an impairment in carrying out the normal day-to-day activity (this should be compared with a person who does not have the impairment)

- the way in which an activity is carried out

- cumulative effects (eg several minor effects of a condition could, taken together, create a substantial adverse effect)

- effects of behaviour (eg can a person modify his behaviour to prevent the effects of an impairment)

- effects of environment (eg temperature or stress)

- effects of treatment – where an impairment is being treated, the impairment is to be considered as having the effect it would have without the treatment. (This does not apply to poor sight where it is corrected by glasses or contact lenses.)

Under schedule 1 of the DDA, where a person has a progressive condition, eg cancer, multiple sclerosis or HIV infection, he is treated as having an impairment that has a substantial adverse effect from the moment he experiences *some* effect on his ability to carry out day-to-day activities, whether the effect is substantial or not.

In the case of *Wallis* v *Action For Employment Limited* (1999, unreported, 1801049/99) Mrs Wallis was employed as administration manager for the employer. In October 1998 she was diagnosed with breast cancer and underwent surgery, chemotherapy and radiotherapy. Her employer refused to allow her to return to work as administration manager and gave her menial work as an options matcher, and recruited another administration manager. Mrs Wallis issued a tribunal application on the basis she had been unlawfully discriminated against because of her disability. The employer argued that her illness did not amount to a disability because it did not have a substantial, long-term adverse effect and it did not affect her ability to carry out normal day-to-day activities. The employment tribunal found that Mrs Wallis was disabled within the meaning of the DDA. Her condition was likely to last for the rest of her life (surgery being undertaken with consequent scarring). But for the chemotherapy and radiotherapy, Mrs Wallis had an impairment that was likely to have a substantial adverse effect on her ability to carry out normal day-to-day activities. Clearly the tribunal was prepared to accept that surgery, chemotherapy and radiotherapy, ie treatments that had been undergone, were still to be disregarded in deciding whether or not the applicant had an impairment that would have a substantial adverse effect on her ability to carry out day-to-day activities.

Severe disfigurements are also treated as having a substantial adverse effect, without the need to show the effect. Therefore individuals with scars, birthmarks etc are potentially covered by the DDA. Under the DDA Guidance, assessing severity will be a matter of degree; for example, it will be material to know whether the mark is on the individual's face or back. The effect or severity will clearly be greater if the mark is on the individual's face.

Long term

Under schedule 1 of the DDA an impairment will be treated as long term and therefore within the definition of disability only if:

- it has lasted at least 12 months

- the period for which it lasts is likely to be at least 12 months

- it is likely to last for the rest of the life of the person affected.

For example, in the case of *Hill* v *Lister-Petter Ltd* (Case No. 1400187/98) the employee was diagnosed as suffering from depression in June 1997. Although the tribunal stated that her depression amounted to a 'clinically well-recognised' illness, which had a substantial effect on her day-to-day activities, the effect of her depression was not long term. Her impairment, therefore, did not fall under the definition of disability.

If a person has had an impairment that at one time had a substantial adverse effect but that ceased, then the substantial effect will be treated as continuing where it is more likely than not to recur. The Guidance gives the example of an individual suffering from rheumatoid arthritis who may have periods of remission. If the effects of the impairment are likely to recur they are treated as if they were continuing.

It is not necessary for the effect of the impairment to be the same throughout the relevant period. The effect may change or disappear even temporarily, but there would still be a long-term effect if the impairment continued to have, or was likely to have, such an effect throughout the period.

The case of *Greenwood* v *British Airways plc* [1999] IRLR 600 EAT tackles the meaning of discrimination in relation to recurring conditions. The applicant, a senior cargo assistant, suffered from depression but, with medical advice, drugs, counselling and the co-operation of management, he was able to return to his full work schedule. He applied for a promotion, which he did not achieve because of his absence. The question before the tribunal was whether he was disabled. Although he was still on anti-depressants and needed counselling, the tribunal decided he was no longer disabled and the impairment was unlikely to recur. The Employment Appeal Tribunal (EAT) overturned this and stated that the tribunal should have taken into account events after the discriminatory event right up to the tribunal hearing and that, because the problem did recur, he was disabled. The EAT stated that, as the Guidance makes clear, the tribunal should have considered the adverse effects of the applicant's condition up to and including the tribunal hearing. By disregarding its findings of fact as to the actual recurrence of the applicant's condition which led him to go off work and to continue off work until the date of the tribunal, the tribunal's approach was fatally flawed.

Normal day-to-day activities

This means activities that are normal for most people, rather than specialised activities such as playing a musical instrument or a particular sport. Under schedule 1 paragraph 4 of the DDA an impairment will affect the ability to carry out normal day-to-day activities where it affects one or more of the items listed below. The examples for each listed item are not exhaustive and, in accordance with the DDA, are meant to be only illustrative:

- *mobility*, eg inability to travel a short journey as a passenger in a vehicle, inability to walk other than at a slow pace or with unsteady or jerky movements

- *manual dexterity*, eg inability to handle a knife and fork or to press buttons on a keyboard

- *physical co-ordination*, eg ability to pour liquid into another vessel only with unusual slowness or concentration

- *continence*, eg loss of control of the bladder while asleep, at least once a month

- *ability to lift, carry or otherwise move everyday objects*, eg inability to carry a moderately loaded tray steadily

- *speech, hearing or eyesight*, eg inability to ask specific questions to clarify instructions, inability to hear and understand another person speaking clearly over the telephone, inability to read ordinary newspaper print

- *memory or ability to concentrate, learn or understand*, eg inability to adapt after a reasonable period to a minor change in work routine, or persistent inability to remember the names of familiar people such as family or friends

- *perception of the risk of physical danger*, eg persistent inability to cross a road safely or inability to tell by touch that an object is very hot or very cold.

A useful case that gave welcome guidance on how to approach section 1, identify the four conditions for satisfying the definition of disability and guide tribunals is the case of *Goodwin* v *The Patent Office* [1999]

IRLR 4. The applicant was a paranoid schizophrenic who was dismissed following complaints from work colleagues about his odd behaviour. The applicant experienced 'thought-broadcasting' and auditory hallucinations. The tribunal took the view that the applicant did not have a disability because the effect of the impairment was not substantial in that the applicant could still care for himself and get to work and carry that out to a satisfactory standard. The applicant appealed. The EAT held that the applicant did have a disability under the DDA. He was unable to provide his employer with a regular and effective service and he was unable to hold a normal conversation (good evidence that the applicant's ability to concentrate and communicate had been adversely affected to a significant degree). The EAT in its guidance to tribunals stated that a purposive approach should be adopted to the interpretation of the legislation and regard should be had to the ordinary and natural meaning of the words, and account should be taken of the provisions of the statutory guidance. The EAT stated that the statute requires a tribunal to look at the evidence by reference to all four of the following different conditions, namely:

- Does the applicant have an impairment that is either physical or mental?

- Does the impairment affect the applicant's ability to carry out normal day-to-day activities and does it have an adverse effect?

- Is the adverse effect substantial?

- Is the adverse effect long term?

Conditions that have been held to amount to a disability

Examples of conditions that have been held by a tribunal to be conditions capable of amounting to a disability include:

- chronic fatigue syndrome or ME (*O'Neill* v *Symm* [1998] IRLR 233)

- asthma (*Cox* v *Post Office* 23.10.97 Case No. 1301162/97)

- epilepsy (*Ridout* v *TC Group* EAT 13.7.98(1371/97))

- cerebral palsy (*Kenny* v *Hampshire Constabulary* EAT 14.10.98 (267/98)

- depression being treated by Prozac (*Toffell* v *London Underground* 9.1.98 Case No. 2204880/97).

Such conditions will not always amount to a disability. It will be a question of fact for the tribunal in each case to determine whether the condition has a substantial and long-term adverse effect on the ability to carry out normal day-to-day activities.

Medical reports will play a crucial role in determining whether an applicant has a disability; but the EAT emphasised in *Vicary* v *British Telecommunications plc* [1999] IRLR 680 that it is for the employment tribunal rather than expert medical witnesses to determine what a normal day-to-day activity is and what should be regarded as a substantial effect.

The power to make regulations features prominently throughout the DDA. Regulations may be made to make provisions for the purposes of the DDA for the following:

- conditions of a prescribed description to be treated as amounting to or not amounting to an impairment

- for prescribing circumstances in which the effect of an impairment is or is not to be treated as a long-term effect

- for prescribing circumstances in which the likelihood of a recurrence of a substantial adverse effect is to be disregarded

- for prescribing circumstances in which an impairment is to be taken to affect the ability to carry out normal day-to-day activities.

The scope and meaning of discrimination

Who is liable? – *Employers – Partnerships – Contract workers – Trade unions and professional and trade organisations – Trustees and managers of occupational pension schemes – Aiding unlawful acts –* Exclusions – *Small businesses – Charities – Overseas employment – Statutory authority – Contracting out –* The meaning of discrimination – Justification

The purpose of this chapter is to identify who is liable for discrimination in employment and to examine the meaning of discrimination. The provisions governing discrimination against disabled people in employment are contained in Part II of the DDA.

WHO IS LIABLE?

Employers

An employer is the main category. Not all employers are covered. Employers with fewer than 15 employees are exempt from the employment provisions (see below). Employment is defined under section 68(1) of the DDA as 'employment under a contract of service or of apprenticeship or a contract personally to do any work.' As a general rule, the DDA applies to the Crown and Crown employment as it does to private employers. Exceptions to this include prison officers, firefighters, the police and members of the armed services.

Under section 58(1) of the DDA employers are also liable for anything done by a person in the course of his employment, whether or not it was done with the employer's knowledge or approval (vicarious liability). An employer will have a defence to a claim if he is able to show that he took reasonable steps to prevent the employee from carrying out the unlawful act. An employer will be assisted in this by having an effective and well-communicated equal opportunities policy or disabled workers policy or both (see page xiv).

Partnerships

Employment by a partnership is protected, although the relationship between partners is not covered.

Contract workers

Section 12 of the DDA covers discrimination against contract workers. A contract worker is any individual who is employed by one party (the agency) but supplied under a contract to another (the principal), eg temporary secretaries or information technology (IT) contract workers. Protection extends to discrimination by the principal as follows:

- in the terms on which the worker is allowed to do the work

- by not allowing him to work or continue working

- in the way the worker is afforded access to benefits, or refusing or deliberately omitting to afford him access

- subjecting the worker to any other detriment.

The small employer exemption also applies to the principal. The calculation includes both the principal's own employees and the contract workers. Principals will also be liable for the discriminatory acts of their agents where the acts were done with the principal's authority. The recent case of *MHC Consulting Services* v *Tansell & ors* EAT 14.9.99 (1378/98) has examined the scope of section 12 of the DDA. In this case the applicant was an IT contractor. He was employed by his own company (I Ltd), which had been set up to limit his liability in the event of his making a negligent mistake in the course of his contract work. The applicant was registered with an employment agency (MHC). The agency found the applicant a placement with a company, AL (the principal). After a period of time the company refused to continue to offer work to the applicant. The applicant believed this was because of his disability and made a complaint of discrimination. The question for the EAT was whether the arrangement in this case fell within the scope of section 12 so as to protect the worker from disability discrimination. The EAT held that where there is an unbroken chain of contracts between an individual and the end-user, the end-user is the principal. So, in this case the applicant could sue AL as the principal. The agency was not the principal because it was not the end-user. The EAT made clear in this case that the decision was based on affording the applicant the protection that social legislation of this kind gives and had erred towards conferring protection rather than excluding it. At the time of writing leave has been given to the parties to appeal.

Trade unions and professional and trade organisations

This means trade unions and organisations such as the Institute of Personnel and Development and the Law Society. Discrimination is prohibited in the terms offered to admit the person to membership, refusal to accept an application, access to any benefits, or subjecting the person to any other form of detriment. In the case of *Sheen* v *The Writers' Guild of Great Britain* [1998] (Case No. 36669/96) Mr Sheen, a writer, was diagnosed as schizophrenic in the mid-1980s. While in a delusional state he had written letters to Ms Banks, the assistant general secretary of the trade union, which were disturbing and distressing. Thereafter his condition was controlled and again he applied for union membership and again was refused following concerns expressed by Ms Banks. He applied again, openly asserting that he was schizophrenic. He continued to be excluded until May 1997 when, following a meeting with the union, any fears on the union's part concerning his condition were dispelled. He complained that the union had unlawfully discriminated against him on grounds of disability by refusing him membership to the union, contrary to section 13(1)(b) of the DDA. The union attempted to justify Mr Sheen's exclusion on the basis that there was a risk of his repeating his previous behaviour. This was rejected by the tribunal, which stated that no investigation had been carried out and any enquiry would have shown that this was an exaggeration. The tribunal awarded £4,000 for injury to feelings.

Trustees and managers of occupational pension schemes

A non-discrimination rule is inserted into every occupational pension scheme, which prohibits managers or trustees of the scheme from carrying out any discriminatory acts in the provision of the scheme and the terms on which members of the scheme are treated.

Aiding unlawful acts

A person who knowingly aids another person to do an act made unlawful by the DDA is to be treated as if he too did the unlawful act.

EXCLUSIONS

Small businesses

In December 1997 the Government reviewed the small-firm exemption which excludes the application of the employment provisions of the DDA where fewer than a certain number of people are employed by an employer. The threshold was reduced from 20 to 15 by the Disability Discrimination (Exemption for Small Employers) Order 1998 with effect from 1 December 1998.

Charities

Charities that determine how to confer benefits on individuals by reference to physical or mental capacity are not be affected by the DDA employment provisions.

Overseas employment

Only employment at an establishment in Great Britain is protected. Where an employee does his work wholly or mainly outside Great Britain his employment will not be treated as being work at an establishment in Great Britain.

Statutory authority

An act that would normally be treated as being unlawful is not so treated where it is in pursuance of an enactment or any condition or requirement imposed by a minister of the Crown or if the act was done to safeguard national security.

Contracting out

Any provision that attempts to contract out of the provisions of the DDA or limit its operation is void.

THE MEANING OF DISCRIMINATION

Section 4 of the DDA sets out the circumstances in which discrimination can occur in the field of employment (see Chapter 3 for particular examples). The Code of Practice ('the Code') issued by the Secretary of State for Education and Employment on 25 July 1996 gives practical guidance to help employers eliminate discrimination both in recruitment and during employment. The Code was issued under section 53(1)(a) of the DDA and, although its provisions do not impose legal obligations, its provisions are admissible in evidence in any proceedings under the DDA before an employment tribunal or court.

Section 4(1) states:

> *It is unlawful for an employer to discriminate against a disabled person:*
>
> *(a) in the arrangements which he makes for the purpose of determining to whom he should offer employment*
>
> *(b) in the terms on which he offers that person employment*
>
> *(c) by refusing to offer, or deliberately not offering, him employment.*

(This covers the area of recruitment and covers job applicants.)

Section 4(2) states:

> *It is unlawful for an employer to discriminate against a disabled person whom he employs*
>
> *(a) in the terms of employment which he affords him*
>
> *(b) in the opportunities which he affords him for promotion, a transfer, training or receiving any other benefit*
>
> *(c) by refusing to afford him, or deliberately not affording him, any such opportunity; or*
>
> *(d) by dismissing him, or subjecting him to any other detriment.*

Discrimination can occur in one of three ways:

* direct discrimination

- discrimination by way of the employer's failure to comply with the duty to make adjustments (see Chapter 4)

- discrimination by way of victimisation.

The first two types of discrimination may be defended by the employer by showing that the treatment is justified (see below). There is no concept of indirect discrimination under the DDA.

Under section 5(1) of the DDA, an employer unlawfully discriminates against a disabled person if:

(a) for a reason that *relates to* the disabled person's disability he treats him *less favourably* than he treats or would treat others to whom that reason does not or would not apply; and

(b) he cannot show that the treatment in question is justified.

The case of *Clark* v *TDG t/a Novacold Ltd* [1999] IRLR 318 has clarified the correct comparator to use in determining whether less favourable treatment has occurred. In July 1995 Mr Clark started work with Novacold in a job that involved strenuous manual work. He suffered a back injury in August 1996 and as a result was not able to work. He was dismissed in January 1997. One of his claims under the DDA was that his dismissal was contrary to section 5 of the DDA, on the basis that the reason for his long absence from work was his disability and that therefore the employer, by dismissing him, had treated him less favourably than a person to whom that reason did not apply. The Court of Appeal (CA) ruled that when the question of less favourable treatment is being considered an employment tribunal must make the comparison *without regard to the disability or its consequences*. In other words, in Mr Clark's case *comparison was with someone to whom the disability-related reason (ie absence) did not apply*, ie someone who was not off sick. The onus is then placed on the employer to show that the treatment is justified (see below). It may be difficult, especially in sickness cases, for an employer to show justification. This will be the case particularly where there is no financial burden caused by the employee's absence, eg because there is no ongoing sick pay obligations. The concept of discrimination under the DDA and the determination of less favourable treatment differs dramatically from the approach adopted under the SDA or RRA.

Following the Clark case, tribunals should now adopt a three-stage test:

1 Identify the reason for the treatment afforded to the disabled person.

2 Identify whether that reason relates to that person's disability.

3 Compare the treatment afforded to the employee with the way in which an employer would treat a person to whom the reason for that treatment would not apply.

This decision has vast implications for employers, because it will be easier for an applicant to show that there has been less favourable treatment. The emphasis will now be on whether the treatment is justified.

JUSTIFICATION

The DDA allows an employer to discriminate if he is able to justify the treatment. Again, the DDA is different in this respect from the SDA and the RRA, which allow the defence of justification only where the claim is one of *indirect* discrimination. There is no concept of indirect discrimination under the DDA. In light of the decision in *Clark*, justification will be the crux of the DDA. Under section 5(3) of the DDA, less favourable treatment can be justified only where:

- the reason for the treatment is both material to the circumstances of the particular case and substantial (ie is not trivial or minor)

- the employer is under a duty to make a reasonable adjustment but fails to comply with that duty; that failure is justified if the reason for it is both material to the circumstances of the case and substantial

- less favourable treatment cannot be justified where the employer is under a duty to make a reasonable adjustment but fails (without justification) to do so, unless that treatment would have been justified even if the duty to make a reasonable adjustment under section 6 had been complied with.

Under the Code of Practice, the reason relied upon to show justification has to relate to the individual circumstances in question and not just be trivial or minor. For further information on reasonable adjustments see Chapter 4.

The recent case of *Baynton* v *Saurus General Engineers Limited* [1999] IRLR 604 EAT has examined the question of justification. The case involved an employee who had injured his thumb at work and was assessed as having a 15 per cent disability. His employment was terminated on the grounds of long-term sickness. The EAT held that in applying the test of justification under section 5(3), an employer should warn an employee of the risk of dismissal and find out the up-to-date medical position. The interests and circumstances of both the employer and employee will be taken into consideration by the tribunal, which, the EAT stated, accorded with the approach taken when considering the question of dismissal for some other substantial reason (SOSR) in the law of unfair dismissal. It follows from the decision in this case that where an employer fails to follow basic principles of good employment practice, such as getting reports on the up-to-date medical position, it is unlikely the tribunal's decision will come out in the employer's favour.

Discrimination in employment

Recruitment – *Advertisements – Job specification – Health requirements – Provision of information and recruitment literature – Application forms – Interviews – Selection and qualifications – Medical examinations – Equality of treatment –* During employment *– Terms and conditions – Induction – Promotion and transfer – Training – Provision of benefits – Pension schemes and insurance – Any other detriment -* Discrimination and dismissal

The purpose of this chapter is to examine the situations in which discrimination may occur during employment. Discrimination can happen at every stage of the employment process, from recruitment through to dismissal. Below is a summary of the issues to consider at each stage. The Code also provides essential guidance. The Code is admissible as evidence in any proceedings under the DDA before a tribunal or court.

RECRUITMENT

Advertisements

There is no prohibition on discriminatory advertisements. However, it could be used to raise a presumption of discrimination where a disabled person has applied for a job and the employer has refused to offer or has deliberately not offered employment. Under section 11 of the DDA the employer must have advertised the employment and the advertisement must have indicated, or might reasonably be understood to have indicated, that any application for the advertised employment would or might be determined to any extent by reference to one or other of the following:

(i) the successful applicant not having a disability or any category of disability which includes the disabled person's disability

(ii) the employer's reluctance to make a reasonable adjustment under section 6 (see Chapter 4).

Employers may, if they wish, have a statement in an advertisement stating that applications are encouraged from disabled people.

Job specification

A job specification should be drawn up with care. It should not contain any 'throw-away' comments that could be discriminatory. In the Code, the example given is of an employer requiring the candidate to be energetic when the job is largely sedentary. Candidates who suffer from disabilities that may cause tiredness would be excluded, without justification, from applying for the role.

In the case of *Murphy* v *Sec Ltd* (1998, unreported), Mrs Murphy was employed as a recruitment consultant. Every other Wednesday she left work early to attend hospital for transfusions necessitated by her condition (hypogammaglobulinaemia), the effect of which was that she generally became more tired. The company was aware of her condition. Staff were called upon to work additional hours, which the applicant did for several weeks, although not all of the hours required. On 7 April 1997 she telephoned the office to say she was feeling sick and would not be coming in that day. She was dismissed, and claimed unlawful discrimination. The tribunal upheld her claim. The reason for the applicant's dismissal was because she was not doing the hours requested. The reason for that was because she was fatigued because of her disability.

Health requirements

An employer may stipulate essential health requirements but will need to be able to show that they are justified. Again, employers should take care not to make 'throw-away' comments which could be potentially discriminatory, such as 'must be in good health'.

Provision of information and recruitment literature

The Code states that the provision of information about a job in other formats, such as Braille or large print, may be considered to be a reasonable adjustment.

Application forms

One of the questions that employers often ask is whether the application form can include a question asking whether the candidate has a disability.

The Code quite clearly states that it is not prohibited to ask whether the candidate has disabilities. From a practical point of view, employers should include a paragraph in the application form stating that the reason the information is requested is in order to investigate whether any reasonable adjustments are required. Employers should also consider the need to provide application forms in different formats to accommodate disabilities (see 'Provision of information', above). An employer will also need to consider allowing potential candidates to submit information in different forms from those which may have been requested in the job advertisement.

Interviews

In the event an employer receives advanced notice of a candidate's disability, the employer should make reasonable adjustments, eg changing lighting, the positioning of chairs in the room, or changing the room the interview is held in; these specific examples are provided for in the Code. Another common question that employers ask is whether it can question an applicant about his disability at the interview. There is no prohibition in the DDA, although any information obtained should not be used in a discriminatory way. The Code gives useful guidance on this area and states that an employer should ask about a disability only if it is relevant to the person's ability to do the job or in considering what reasonable adjustments may need to be made.

Selection and qualifications

Aptitude tests under the DDA are not prohibited, although the effect of them could be discriminatory. The Code gives the example of an employer who sets a numeracy test for prospective employees. A candidate with learning disabilities does not achieve the required standard. If the job requires very little numeracy work and the candidate is otherwise well suited to the job it would be a reasonable adjustment for the employer to waive the requirement. Where the employer requires a particular qualification for the job and a disabled person is rejected because he does not have the qualification, then the employer must be able to justify that the qualification is relevant and significant to the role.

Medical examinations

An employer can require all candidates, including disabled candidates, to undergo a medical examination. A medical check for a disabled person can be required only if justified; otherwise it will be discriminatory.

Equality of treatment

Other than in relation to the requirements of the DDA, there is no requirement to treat a disabled candidate more favourably than others. If the disabled candidate is not the best person for the job (after considering reasonable adjustments) the employer is not under an obligation to recruit him. The flip side is that the DDA does not prohibit positive discrimination, as is the case under the SDA or the RRA.

DURING EMPLOYMENT

Under section 4(2) of the DDA it is unlawful for an employer to discriminate against a disabled person:

- in the terms of the employment that he affords him

- in the opportunities that he affords him for promotion, a transfer, training or receiving any other benefit

- by refusing to afford him, or deliberately not affording him, any such opportunity

- by dismissing him or subjecting him to any other detriment.

The Code provides specific guidance on all areas of discrimination during employment.

Terms and conditions

Terms and conditions should not discriminate against a disabled person, and an employer should consider whether any reasonable adjustments are necessary. Several practical examples are given in the Code, such as adjusting an employee's hours to avoid rush hour for someone who has difficulty in using public transport. A less favourable contract cannot be offered, unless the employer is able to justify it, and there is no reasonable adjustment that can be made to remove the disadvantage leading to that reason.

Induction

The Code states that an employer must not discriminate in his induction procedures, and reasonable adjustments must be made to ensure that a disabled person is introduced into the new working environment in a structured and supported way.

Promotion and transfer

Under section 4(2)(b) of the DDA, an employer must not discriminate in opportunities for promotion, transfer or training, or the receipt of any other benefit. This could cover areas such as selection processes and annual appraisals. An employer will need to consider reasonable adjustments in the processes used, eg in assessing suitability for promotion. The specific example the Code gives is in relation to a candidate who has a hearing impairment. For the purposes of the assessment interview the employer should find out whether the candidate needs any special arrangements, such as a sign language interpreter.

Training

Employers must not discriminate in selection for training. If a disabled person is put at a substantial disadvantage in the arrangements made for training, the employer may have to make reasonable adjustments.

Provision of benefits

Under section 4(4) of the DDA, benefits include facilities and services. According to the Code, benefits might include canteens, meal vouchers, social clubs and other recreational activities, dedicated car parking spaces, discounts on products, bonuses, share options, hairdressing, clothes allowances, financial services, healthcare, medical assistance/insurance, transport to work, a company car, educational assistance, workplace nurseries and rights to special leave. The employer must make any necessary reasonable adjustment to the way the benefits are provided. (This does not apply to benefits under occupational pension schemes – see below.)

Pension schemes and insurance

A non-discrimination rule is inserted into every occupational pension scheme, and under section 17 of the DDA trustees or managers of the scheme are prohibited from doing anything that would be discriminatory. Less favourable treatment on the grounds of a disability will be allowed only where the treatment is justified. The reason must be material and substantial. Justification may be that the cost of providing benefits is substantially greater than it would be for a person without the disability, owing to the disabled person's health or health prognosis. Justification would have to be shown, by actuarial advice or medical evidence, of the substantially increased cost. The argument of justification may be used only at the time of admission to the scheme and applies to occupational pension schemes, termination of service, retirement, old age or death, accident, injury, sickness or invalidity. The duty to make reasonable adjustments (see Chapter 4) does *not* apply to the provision of benefits under an occupational pension scheme or any other benefit payable in money or money's worth under a scheme or arrangement for the benefit of employees in respect of:

- termination of service

- retirement, old age or death

- accident, injury, sickness or invalidity.

Protection under the DDA is extended to the provision of group insurance such as permanent health insurance or life assurance.

Any other detriment

This is a catch-all provision which protects the employee from being put at a disadvantage. The harassment of a disabled employee is stated in the Code to be almost always likely to amount to a detriment. An employer is vicariously liable for the acts of his employees carried out in the course of employment and should have in place a policy clearly stating that harassment is a disciplinary matter (see page xiv for an example of a basic policy).

DISCRIMINATION AND DISMISSAL

A disabled employee who has been dismissed has two possible routes of claim:

- a claim of discrimination under the DDA (the tribunal will identify the reason for less favourable treatment, compare it with the treatment of someone to whom the reason did not or would not apply, and determine whether the dismissal was justified)

- a claim of unfair dismissal under the Employment Rights Act 1996 (ERA). There is a qualifying period of service of one year. (A tribunal will look at the reasonableness of the dismissal.)

One of the main areas affected by the DDA is in relation to ill-health dismissals. Incapability due to long-term ill health can be a fair reason to dismiss as long as a proper procedure is followed. In summary, the basic requirements are these:

1 The employer must be fully apprised of all the facts relating to the employee's medical condition.

2 Generally, a medical report will be required from the employee's GP and/or consultant.

3 The requirements of the Access to Medical Reports Act 1988 must be complied with.

4 Any company sickness procedure must be complied with (especially if contractual).

5 The employee's views must be obtained.

6 Alternative employment to avoid dismissal must be fully considered and enquiries must be documented.

7 Consideration must be made as to whether the illness amounts to a disability.

8 In deciding whether to dismiss, the employer should consider such relevant factors as the importance of the employee's job, the feasibility of a temporary replacement, and the likely length of absence.

9 Employees should have the right to appeal against any decision to dismiss.

However, the tribunal will consider *all* the circumstances of the case. The fact that any particular step set out above is or is not taken by an employer will not necessarily be decisive in determining fairness in any particular case.

In relation to point 7, if the illness *does* amount to a disability then the employer will have to consider further issues. Under the DDA, dismissal is justified only where the reason for dismissal is material and substantial (not trivial or minor) to the circumstances of the case. An employer must also consider whether any substantial disadvantage suffered by the employee can be removed by making a reasonable adjustment (see Chapter 4 and 'Justification' in Chapter 3). The applicability of the duty to make reasonable adjustments under section 6 of the DDA was clarified in the case of *Morse* v *Wiltshire County Council* [1998] IRLR 352. In this case, Mr Morse, following an accident, was left with a 20 per cent disability. Because of his tendency to suffer blackouts he did not drive a vehicle when he returned to work, nor did he work on heights or near water if he was alone, or operate power tools. When the employer needed to make redundancies the applicant's lack of driving ability and the limitations on what he could do led to his selection for redundancy. The EAT held that the duty to make reasonable adjustments under section 6 applies indirectly to a dismissal situation. The employer is under a duty to see whether he can take steps reasonably to avoid dismissing a disabled employee. The EAT also stated that the duty under section 6 applies not only in relation to the employee's current role but also to ensure that any alternative employment be considered in order to avoid dismissal. This may mean additional training or increased assistance in getting used to the role. The Code gives examples of rearranging working methods, practical aids or adaptations to equipment or premises.

The DDA is also relevant in the selection of candidates in a redundancy situation. Employers should take care not only to use objective criteria to select potential candidates but also that none of the criteria chosen causes an element of discrimination, eg the use of records relating to attendance, productivity and/or health. The use of selection criteria that are potentially discriminatory will have to be justified, ie be material to the particular circumstances of the case and be substantial.

The duty to make reasonable adjustments

What are 'arrangements'? – What are 'physical features'? – *Steps that an employer may have to take – When is it reasonable to make an adjustment? – The effect of the Building Regulations – Statutory consent – Landlord consent – Excluded categories – Service providers' duty to make reasonable adjustments*

The purpose of this chapter is to summarise the provisions in relation to the duty of the employer to make reasonable adjustments.

The employer's obligations are contained in section 6 of the DDA. The duty is to take such steps as are reasonable to prevent *any arrangements* made by him or on his behalf, or any *physical features* of the employer's premises, from placing a disabled applicant or employee at a *substantial disadvantage* (ie not minor or trivial) compared with those applicants or employees who are not disabled. If the employer fails to comply with this duty, then such failure, where it cannot be justified, amounts under section 5(2) to discrimination against the disabled person. The failure can be justified only if the reason for the failure is both material in the circumstances and is substantial (see Chapter 3 for information on justification). The duty to make reasonable adjustments also applies in relation to the principals of contract workers, trade unions, and professional, trade and employers' organisations.

WHAT ARE 'ARRANGEMENTS'?

Under section 6(2) of the DDA, 'arrangements' mean:

- any arrangements made for determining to whom employment should be offered

- any term, condition or arrangement on which employment, promotion, a transfer, training or any other benefit is offered or afforded.

This means that the employer will be required to make adjustments in relation to the arrangements for recruitment and during employment.

This may include interview and selection procedures, job offers, contractual arrangements and working conditions.

WHAT ARE 'PHYSICAL FEATURES'?

The meaning of 'physical features' is set out in regulation 9 of the Disability Discrimination (Employment) Regulations 1996, which states that the items listed below are to be treated as physical features:

- any feature arising from the design or construction of a building (ie erection or structure of any kind) on the premises

- any feature on the premises of any approach to, exit from, or access to such a building

- any fixtures fittings, furnishings, furniture, equipment or materials in or on the premises

- any other physical element or quality of any land comprised in the premises.

Steps that an employer may have to take

Section 6(3) of the DDA gives practical examples of steps that an employer may have to take in order to comply with his duty to make reasonable adjustments. These are:

- making adjustments to premises (eg widening a doorway for a wheelchair)

- allocating some of the disabled person's duties to another person

- transferring him to fill an existing vacancy

- altering his working hours (eg giving more flexible hours)

- assigning him to a different place of work

- allowing him to be absent during working hours for rehabilitation, assessment or treatment (eg physiotherapy)

- giving him, or arranging for him to be given, training

- acquiring or modifying equipment (eg adapting a keyboard)

- modifying instructions or reference manuals (eg Braille or audio tape)

- modifying procedures for testing or assessment

- providing a reader or interpreter (eg sign language)

- providing supervision (eg a support worker).

When is it reasonable to make an adjustment?

Section 6(4) of the DDA lists a number of factors that may be considered in determining whether it is reasonable for an employer to make an adjustment. They are:

- the extent to which taking the step would prevent the effect in question (where there is little benefit to the disabled employee it is unlikely to be reasonable for the employer to have to make an adjustment)

- the extent to which it is practicable for the employer to take the step (an employer should consider making temporary adjustments while a long-term adjustment is made, eg to an entrance)

- the financial and other costs that would be incurred by the employer in taking the step and the extent to which taking it would disrupt any of his activities (the costs an employer can take into account include the costs of staff and other resource costs; also of consideration is the value of the employee's experience and expertise)

- the extent of the employer's financial and other resources (it is likely to be more reasonable for a larger employer with greater financial resources to make a significant adjustment than a smaller employer with fewer resources)

- the availability to the employer of financial or other assistance with respect to taking the step (where grants and assistance are available it is likely to be reasonable for the employer to make the adjustment).

Case examples of reasonable adjustments include a blind teacher who was entitled to the help of a classroom assistant (*Abbott* v *The Governors of St Mary's Catholic Primary School* Case No. 3204241/97), a nursing assistant who should have been transferred to clerical/secretarial duties (*Angel* v *New Possibilities NHS Trust* Case No. 1501552/98), and a business support manager whose office should have been relocated to the ground floor to avoid the need to climb stairs each day (*Fletcher* v *Turning Point* Case No. 1300613/98).

An example of an unsuccessful claim by an applicant is provided by the case of *Ridout* v *TC Group* EAT 13.7.98 (1371/97). The EAT ruled that an employer did not discriminate against an interviewee with a rare form of epilepsy that was affected by light when he failed to make any adjustment to the lighting in an office that was to be used for interviewing the prospective employee. The employer was unaware that any adjustment was required and, in any event, the interviewee was not put at a substantial disadvantage.

The extent of the duty to make reasonable adjustments was recently demonstrated in the case of *London Borough of Hillingdon* v *Morgan* EAT 27.5.99 (1493/98). Mrs Morgan was employed as a service information officer and had ME. She took sick leave, and eight months later her GP and occupational health doctor suggested that she ease herself gradually back into the work routine, preferably starting off part-time. The applicant returned to work but no arrangements were made for her care or support; she resigned because she could not cope with the stress of her job, bringing a claim of disability discrimination. The EAT held that the employer had failed to comply with the duty to make adjustments by not allowing an employee who had become disabled to work from home temporarily, to assist her to ease back into full-time work. The clear message from the EAT is that an adjustment may be reasonable under the DDA if an employer's financial and administrative resources make it feasible.

The effect of the Building Regulations

The Disability Discrimination (Employment) Regulations 1996 deal with the duty to make reasonable adjustments in relation to the Building Regulations 1991. Where the conditions set out below are met it will never be reasonable for an employer to have to make an adjustment involving the alteration of any physical characteristic of a building. The conditions are as follows:

- The physical characteristics of the building must have been constructed in accordance with Part M of the Building Regulations or Part T of the Technical Standard Regulations in Scotland with regard to access and facilities for disabled people.

- The buildings must have met those requirements at the time the building work was carried out.

- The building must continue substantially to meet those requirements as they applied at the time the work was carried out.

Statutory consent

In some circumstances an employer may have to obtain statutory consents, such as planning permission, before making some changes to buildings. Where statutory consent has been refused, the employer is not obliged to make an adjustment, although the employer may be under an obligation to investigate ways of making adjustments that do not require consent.

Landlord consent

If an employer is required under the terms of a lease to obtain landlord consent to make adjustments to premises, then special provisions apply under section 16 of the DDA. These state that the employer must write to the landlord asking for consent. If consent is granted, the alteration may be carried out. If the landlord refuses consent, the employer must inform the disabled person. Where the landlord fails to reply within a period of 21 days he is deemed to have withheld his consent. Regulation 13 sets out the circumstances in which a landlord will be deemed to be reasonable in withholding consent, and the Code gives the examples of where the adjustment is likely to result in a substantial permanent reduction in the value of the landlord's interest in the premises, or where a particular adjustment would cause significant disruption or inconvenience to other tenants. A landlord may give his consent conditionally, or in some circumstances he may be subject to further consent from a superior landlord.

If a subsequent tribunal claim is made against the employer for breach of his duty to make a reasonable adjustment where section 16 applies, then either the employer or the disabled applicant may ask the tribunal to join the landlord as a party to the proceedings. If the tribunal considers that consent has been unreasonably withheld, the tribunal may make a declaration and order that the alteration be made and make an award of compensation against the landlord.

Other consents required may include those in relation to mortgages and restrictive covenants.

Excluded categories

Those excluded from the duty to make reasonable adjustments are trustees and managers in relation to the provision of benefits under an occupational pension scheme or any other benefit payable in money or money's worth under a scheme or arrangement for the benefit of employees in respect of termination of service, retirement, old age or death, accident, injury, sickness or invalidity. This also includes the provision of occupational insurance benefits relating to the matters above.

Service providers' duty to make reasonable adjustments

Under Part III of the DDA, service providers have a new duty to make reasonable adjustments for disabled people in the way they provide their services. The duty will be fully in force from 2004, but the majority of the provisions were brought into effect on 1 October 1999. The new duties will impinge on employers because nearly all service providers will be employers and, as such, are responsible for the acts of their employees in the course of their employment. Employers will need to establish and monitor discrimination policies and train their employees in the requirements of the DDA. Educating staff is a priority that employers should not ignore. A Code of Practice has been produced, which gives guidance on steps geared to the duty of adjustments:

- auditing physical and non-physical barriers to access for disabled people

- making adjustments and putting them in place

- giving staff relevant training on adjustments

- drawing adjustments to the attention of disabled people

- letting disabled people know how to request assistance

- regularly reviewing the effectiveness of adjustments.

Enforcement

The questionnaire procedure – Settlement – The
Disability Rights Commission

Section 8(1) of the DDA states that an employment tribunal has
jurisdiction to hear complaints about unlawful discrimination under the
DDA. The purpose of this chapter is to look briefly at the rules of
enforcement.

The time limit for the presentation of a case of discrimination is three
months from the time that the act complained of was done. A tribunal
may consider a complaint that is out of time if, in all the circumstances
of the case, it considers it just and equitable to do so. In deciding when
the act complained of was done, the following applies:

- Where the act is attributable to a term in the contract, that act is
  to be treated as extending through the duration of the contract.

- Any act extending over a period shall be treated as having been
  done at the end of that period.

- A deliberate omission shall be treated as having been done when
  the person in question decided upon it.

In the event that a claim is well founded, the tribunal shall take such
steps as it considers just and equitable, as follows:

- Make a declaration as to the rights of the complainant and the
  respondent in relation to the matters to which the complaint
  relates.

- Order the respondent to pay compensation to the complainant.
  Compensation may include compensation for injury to feelings.
  There is no upper limit on compensation and the award may
  include interest.

- Recommend that the respondent take, within a specified period, action appearing to the tribunal to be reasonable in the circumstances for the purpose of obviating or reducing the adverse effect on the complainant of any matter to which the complaint relates. Failure, without reasonable justification, to comply with such a recommendation may lead to an increase in the amount of compensation to be paid if such an increase is considered by the tribunal to be just and equitable.

According to a report by the Equal Opportunities Review in 1998 – the second full year of the operation of the DDA – employment tribunals awarded total compensation of £253,030, a sevenfold increase on the previous year. One of the biggest awards was in the case of *Kirker* v *British Sugar plc* (Case No. 2601249/97). A Nottingham tribunal awarded compensation of £102,717 (plus interest) to a visually impaired chemist who was discriminated against when selected for redundancy. The bulk of the award was for future loss. The tribunal based its calculation on the assumption that Mr Kirker would not find alternative employment for the rest of his working life (15 years).

The recent case of *Sheriff* v *Klyne Tugs Ltd* (24 June 1999) may also have a significant impact on damages in discrimination. Abbanur Sheriff, a Muslim, was employed as an engineer and claimed during his employment that he suffered racial harassment and abuse, as a result of which he had a nervous breakdown. Mr Sheriff brought a complaint of race discrimination in the employment tribunal, which was settled. He subsequently brought a claim in the county court for damages for personal injury caused by the abusive treatment he had received from the employer. The claim was initially struck out on the basis it had already been compromised because tribunals had the power to award damages for personal injury. On appeal it was held that the employment tribunal had jurisdiction to award compensation by way of damages for personal injury, including both physical and psychiatric injury caused by the statutory tort of unlawful discrimination. This decision has the practical effect of establishing a new potential head of damages in discrimination cases. If an applicant can show that he has been discriminated against unlawfully and as a result has suffered a personal injury, then the employment tribunal may award compensation for it. Applicants will need to obtain medical reports if they want to claim injury to health. From a tactical point of view, as in the Sherrif case, an applicant who does not claim damages in the employment tribunal will be barred from bringing a claim in the ordinary courts unless he first launchs personal injury proceedings in the ordinary courts. It is likely that damages under this head could be substantial.

THE QUESTIONNAIRE PROCEDURE

Where a person believes he may have been discriminated against, he can submit a questionnaire to the alleged discriminator. This is already an established procedure within the SDA and the RRA. The procedure may be used as a way of establishing a claim and be used in evidence at the tribunal or may be used as a means of obtaining further evidence after the tribunal application has been made. In the event the alleged discriminator either fails to reply or fails to do so within a reasonable period of time, the tribunal may draw any inference it considers just and equitable to draw.

SETTLEMENT

As with other claims of discrimination, the claim may be settled either via a valid compromise agreement under section 9 of the DDA or via ACAS. Any term in a contract that excludes or limits the operation of any provision of the DDA, or prevents the presentation of a complaint to an employment tribunal, is void.

THE DISABILITY RIGHTS COMMISSION

The Disability Rights Commission Bill received Royal Assent on 28 July 1999. The Commission will:

- work towards eliminating discrimination against disabled people

- promote equal opportunities for disabled people

- provide information and advice, particularly to disabled people, employers and service providers

- prepare codes of practice and encourage good practice

- keep the working of the DDA under review

- investigate discrimination and ensure compliance with the law

- arrange for a conciliation service between service providers and disabled people to help in disputes in regard to access to goods and services.

Future developments

Clearly, the DDA is a unique piece of anti-discriminatory legislation, which continues to be interpreted by the tribunals. The DDA has now been in operation for three years and its impact is clearly being felt in the workplace. Applications to employment tribunals are increasing, which is acting as an impetus for employers either to implement or to review existing policies for discrimination.

The establishment of the Disability Rights Commission, which should be in place by April 2000, will provide an adequate enforcement provision, the lack of which has been the subject of much criticism. The Disability Rights Commission will have powers similar to those of the Equal Opportunities Commission (EOC) or the Commission for Racial Equality (CRE). The duties of the Commission will be to work towards the elimination of discrimination against disabled people, to promote the equalisation of opportunities for disabled people and to keep under review the DDA and the forthcoming Disability Rights Commission Act.

The Commission will have the same rights as the EOC and the CRE to conduct formal investigations in order to determine whether unlawful discrimination has taken or is taking place. The most significant benefit to disabled people will be that it may give legal assistance to individuals who have complained or who are proposing to complain to an employment tribunal that they have been discriminated against.

A report by the Disability Rights Task Force (DRTF) was also published in December 1999. Key recommendations by the DRTF include these:

- The threshold for the small employer of 15 employees should be lowered to those employers with fewer than two employees.

- The DDA provisions should be consistent with the SDA and the RRA and be extended to partnerships, qualifying bodies, statutory officeholders, police and prison officers, firefighters, the armed forces, barristers, advocates and victimised ex-employees.

- In recruitment, disability-related enquiries should be permitted, where justified, only once a job offer, conditional on passing a medical or other test, has been made.

- Employment tribunals should be able to order reinstatement or re-engagement of disabled people whom they find to have been unlawfully discriminated against by being dismissed.

The recommendations are currently being considered by the Government.

Developments from Europe are also likely to provide further assistance to disabled people. The Treaty of Amsterdam, signed on 2 October 1997, includes a new article 13. Article 13 provides for 'appropriate action to combat discrimination based on sex, racial or ethnic origin, religion or belief, disability, age or sexual orientation'. A draft framework directive based upon this article is currently being prepared by the European Commission and will in the future provide further protection.

Clearly, the law relating to disability discrimination continues to grow and develop. Employers will need to work hard to keep up to date with new laws and put into practice the new culture in the workplace.

Legal Essentials

The *Legal Essentials* series is a set of practical reference books specially written for human resource practitioners who need answers to all their employment law questions and for lawyers working in the field of employment law.

New or forthcoming legislation is always a source of anxiety to anyone with responsibility for those in the workplace. This series is especially designed to quell this anxiety and will answer all your questions on topics of current interest – particularly on troublesome issues, including subjects where there is a substantial body of case-law.

Written by the CIPD's employment law advisers, Hammond Suddards Edge, the *Legal Essentials* series provides instantly accessible information that could save you unnecessary legal costs. With recent examples from case-law, check-lists and policy guidelines, *Legal Essentials* will quickly build into an up-to-date library providing all the answers to today's crucial employment-law questions.

About the authors

Hammond Suddards Edge run the popular legal advisory service for CIPD members, a service that takes literally thousands of calls a month from HR practitioners worried about the legal implications of their jobs.

Judith Firth, legal adviser on the CIPD legal advisory service, and **Susan Nickson**, Hammond Suddards Edge partner and head of Hammond Suddards Edge Employment Unit, write from extensive experience of employment law. Judith Firth will also be familiar to CIPD members for her regular column on employment law issues in *People Management* magazine.

Ordering copies

Call Customer Services, Plymbridge Distributors Ltd on 01752 202301.

Please remember: all orders for individual titles or the binder that accompanies the series must include a cheque or credit-card details.

If paying at CIPD members' price, please give your membership number.